Autumn Rhythm

Autumn Rhythm

NEW AND SELECTED POEMS

Leon Stokesbury

THE UNIVERSITY OF ARKANSAS PRESS

FAYETTEVILLE   1996

00   99   98   97   96   5   4   3   2   1

Designed by Ellen Beeler

⊖ The paper used in this publication meets the minimum requirements of the American
National Standard for Permanence of Paper for Printed Library Materials Z39.48-1984.

Library of Congress Cataloging-in-Publication Data

Stokesbury, Leon, 1945–
    Autumn rhythm : new and selected poems / Leon Stokesbury.
        p. cm.
    Includes bibliographical references (p.).
    ISBN 1-55728-437-7 (cloth : alk. paper). — ISBN 1-55728-438-5 (paper : alk. paper)
    I. Title.
    PS3569.T6223A94   1996   95-52060
    811'.54—dc20   CIP

for Susan and Erin

Acknowledgments

Many of the poems in *Autumn Rhythm* have been selected from *Often in Different Landscapes* (Austin, 1976), copyright 1976 by Leon Stokesbury; *The Drifting Away of All We Once Held Essential* (Denton, 1979) limited edition, copyright 1979 by Leon Stokesbury; *The Royal Nonesuch* (Tallahassee, 1984) limited edition, copyright 1984 by Leon Stokesbury; *The Drifting Away* (Fayetteville, 1986) copyright 1986 by Leon Stokesbury.

Grateful acknowledgment is made to the following publications in which some of the poems in *Autumn Rhythm* originally appeared, some in slightly different versions: *Atlanta Review, Barataria Review, Charlotte Poetry Review, Crazyhorse, Georgia Review, Greensboro Review, Intro 2, Kentucky Poetry Review, Kenyon Review, Lowlands Review, Mill Mountain Review, Mississippi Review, New England Review, New Orleans Review, New Virginia Review, New Yorker, Ohio State University Journal, Pacific Review, Partisan Review, Poem, Poetry Northwest, Prairie Schooner, Quarterly West, Quartet Magazine, Red Weather, Shenandoah, Southern Poetry Review, Southern Review, Stone Drum,* and *Swallow's Tale.*

Contents

III. from *The Drifting Away* (1986)

IV.

Time is now fleeting,
The moments are passing,
Passing from you, and from me—

Shadows are gathering,
Death's night is coming,
Coming for you, and for me.

—*"Softly and Tenderly,"*
Will Lamartine Thompson, 1847–1909

"Bilgewater, kin I trust you?" says the old
man, still sort of sobbing.
"To the bitter death!" He took the old
man by the hand and squeezed it, and says,
"The secret of your being: speak!"

—The Adventures of Huckleberry Finn

He supposed this was what life taught you,
that words you thought were a joke,
and applied to someone else,
were real, and applied to you.

—*Louis Simpson*

I

Fall

One lit match and there they go.
Like a revolution.

To jump into that

would be death.

But we are all sane people here.
Here is where
we fight it off
with rakes.

We keep it at bay.

It would mean death.

                      So

soon,
only the white ash is left.

An Inkling

Just two weeks graduated from Central High
in 1942, my mother finds herself
employed as the candy girl
at the State Theatre
in downtown Oklahoma City.
                              And just
across the street, at the Liberty Theatre,
my father, who does not know
my mother yet, is head usher,
although Assistant Manager
is his actual title,
as he is quick to tell.

From where she stands, my mother
sometimes gazes across the street
and sees my father taking tickets,
sweeping, changing the marquee.

He really is a pretty boy,
she thinks. And she
is not alone. All the usherettes
at the State think so too.
And they have all, all that are
in the game anyway, given him
a shot, a little wiggle, the once-over,
the come-on, these last few weeks,
to no avail. Why is that?
My mother does not know.

There is a war on, and there
are Army and Navy boys
everywhere, half of them not much
or no older than herself,
but god, doesn't he look divine

in that navy-blue head usher's uniform,
with gold braid up and down
each arm and pants leg too,
and gold buttons, and epaulets
with gold fringe hanging off.

She thinks how fine they both
might look together on a date,
but her State uniform
is green, pool-table-green,
with dark green braid
and buttons too.
                    Even so,
she loves it. The pants
and jacket make her think
of Dr. Dolittle.
                    She remembers
reading Dr. Dolittle back
ten years before. Her favorite book
had been *Dr. Dolittle and the Secret Lake*
because it was so thick.
It made her blush
when people came up
and remarked how smart
she must be to read
such a big book.
So she read it four times.

But she remembers also
the picture on the cover
with Dr. Dolittle in his pool-
table-green jacket and trousers,
or were they called pantaloons?
She cannot recall.

And then, one week later,
Charlene is out front, and she says
something to my father, and he says
something back, and he smiles.
And when my mother,
from behind the candy counter
and the tinted plate-glass doors,
sees that smile,
that settles things.

Something in that smile.
                                    So
by mid-July she has dropped
her crumbs, she has stood
upwind, she has cast her line,
and he has bit the bait, her hook
now nestled tight against
the inside of his lower lip,
and she is seriously
considering hauling him in.

On their third date he borrows a car,
and after work they go
to Beverly's Drive-In and order
Chicken-in-the-Rough. She spent
weekends and holidays the year before
as a carhop there: Beverly's
is perfect. Beverly's is A-OK.
Beverly's is divine.

Then she shows him a place
out by Indian Stadium
where they can park
and spend some time alone.
They have not worn

their uniforms, and she is glad
she had not asked him to.
                              They stop
at the far end of the stadium
parking lot. The moonlight
shining on the gravel gray
has turned it the color of mercury.
My father turns, and puts his arm
around my mother, and kisses her,
and then he looks down,
and lifts his other hand,
and rests it gently, Oh
so gently, against my mother's
blouse.
              He then applies
a small amount of pressure.
He wants her to see that
he is kind, but firm.
                              And so,
gently, he applies pressure
to her blouse, and thus
to the bra beneath that blouse,
and, thus, to the breast
beneath that bra.
                              And he looks down
into her eyes, questioning. Hesitant,
but firm.
                  And my mother looks
up into the glow and darkness
and sees that question there.
An omen, maybe. An inkling.
And it makes her think, for just
an instant, of her own father, Clyde,
four years back.
                              Clyde had never

questioned, had he? Oh no.
That bourbon-breath on top of her,
that ape-like pawing,
pushing her down, the reek
and stink of whiskey over
everything, and the stumbling off
afterward, off her bed and out
into the kitchen to vomit and pass out
like the pig he was.
                         The next day,
her Mama took her on the bus
eighty-five miles from Weatherford
to Oklahoma City and the good
open arms and home of Aunt Helen.
But then her Mama rode right back
to Weatherford and stayed.
For more than one whole year
she stayed—until Clyde beat
her up and ran off one last time.

So my mother lifts her eyes
and sees that questioning. She notices,
too, a tiny band of platinum—
perspiration—above my father's lip,
for, although it is past midnight,
it stays hot in Oklahoma City
in the summertime.
                         In ten months
my father will be sweating more
with a fever of one hundred and five,
having contracted malaria
on the island of New Guinea,
soon to be sent stateside
as his only cure.

           But now my mother
gazes up at my father's eyes.
I tell you she looks up,
and she sees what is in
my father's eyes, and what
will be in my father's eyes,
and what will never be
in my father's eyes, this once
and future moralist wanting
always to do good, to strive,
to find. This pretty boy.

She drops her gaze again
to see the moon's milk spilt
all down the front of her blouse,
and all over my father's hand
resting, firmly, there.
Then she rests her own hand
on the steering wheel, shifts
slightly, and leans her heavy head
against my father's shoulder.
As she does so, she can feel
the taut muscles along the back
of her neck begin to ease.

She shivers for a second,
then meets his eyes, those obscure
agents of augury, once more.
He is smiling. Such
a gentle face, with such
a gentle smile. And so
she smiles back at him.
And it is in this fashion,
with all the world at war,

that my mother smiles back,
to let my father know that
this will do. This is
satisfactory. This little sphere
inside this Ford at one end
of this empty parking lot
will do for her, she seems
to say, as she glances down again,
with the whole world swirled
in shades of pearl and mercury,
at her breast laved in moonlight,
at my father's hand resting there,
questioning. And it is thus
that she cedes to him,
as though through a scrim
of reverie, that small concession.

Evening's End
1943–1970

For the first time in what must be
the better part of two years now
I happened to hear Janis
in her glory—
all that tinctured syrup
dripping off
a razorblade—
on the radio today singing "Summertime."

And it took me back to this girl I knew,
a woman really, my first year
writing undergraduate poetry
at the Mirabeau B. Lamar
State College of Technology
in Beaumont, Texas,
back in 1966.

This woman was the latest in a line,
the latest steady
of my friend John Coyle that spring—
and I remember she was plain:
she was short: and plain
and wore her brown hair up
in a sort of bun in back
that made her plainer still.

I don't know where John met her,
but word went round
she had moved back in with Mom and Dad
down in Port Arthur
to get her head straight,
to attend Lamar,
to study History,
after several years in San Francisco
where she had drifted

into a "bad scene"
taking heroin.

I was twenty,
still lived with Mom and Dad myself,
and so knew nothing
about "bad scenes,"
but I do remember once or twice
each month that spring
John would give a party
with this woman always there.
And always as the evening's end came on
this woman, silent for hours,
would reveal, from thin air,
her guitar,
settle in a chair,
release her long hair
from the bun it was in,
and begin.

Her hair flowed over her shoulders,
and the ends of the strands of hair
like tarnished brass in lamplight
would brush and drag across
the sides of the guitar
as this woman bent
over it.

How low and guttural, how
slow and torchlit, how
amber her song, how absolutely
unlike the tiny nondescript
a few minutes before.—

And I remember also,
from later on that spring,

from May of that year,
two nights in particular.

The first night was a party
this woman gave
at her parents' home.
Her parents' home
was beige:
the bricks the parents' home
was built with
were beige.
The entire house was carpeted
in beige.

John's girl greeted everyone at the door,
a martini in one hand
and a lit cigarette
in an Oriental
ivory cigarette holder in the other,
laughing
for once, and tossing back
her long brown hair.

All the women wore
black full-length party dresses—
and I remember the young woman's father,
how odd he seemed
in his charcoal suit and tie,
his gray hair—
how unamused.

Then John Coyle was drunk.
He spilled his beer
across the beige frontroom carpet:
that darker dampness sinking in,

the father vanished
from the scene.

The next week we double-dated.
I convinced John and his girl
to see a double feature,
Irma La Douce and *Tom Jones,*
at the Pines Theatre.

And I can recall John's girl
saying just one thing that night.

After the films, John was quizzical,
contentious, full of ridicule
for movies I had guaranteed he would enjoy.
He turned and asked her
what she thought—
and in the softest
of tones, a vague rumor
of honeysuckle in the air,
she almost whispered,
"I thought they were beautiful."

That was the last time that I saw her,
the last thing that I heard her say.

A few weeks later,
she drove over to John's house
in the middle of the afternoon,
and caught him in bed
with Suzanne Morain,
a graduate assistant
from the English Department at Lamar.

John told me later
that when she saw them in the bedroom

she ran into the kitchen,
picked up a broom,
and began to sweep the floor—
weeping.

When John sauntered in
she threw the broom at him,
ran out the door,
got in her car and drove away.
And from that day on,
no one ever saw that woman
in Beaumont again.

The next day she moved to Austin.
And later on, I heard,
back to San Francisco.
And I remember when John told me this,
with a semi-shocked expression
on his face, he turned
and looked up, and said, "You know,
I guess she must have really *loved* me."

I was twenty years old.
What did I know?
What could I say?

I could not think
of anything to say,
except, "Yes,
I guess so."

It was summertime.

Thus runs the world away.

The Garden Path

When my bloodshot eyes
grow tired from reading
all day long, why I just
look how no child comes
down the garden path
with a leaf of grass
and questions; and if
one did, "On the fringes
always, on the fringes,"
I might say. But how
to explain this need
of us and three black
grizzlies skating on ice
drunk, mad to break through
down where waters run? I
could say that, or say
as in other things
only skin deep we get
to go. There's blood
down there, blankness, I
could say if some child
came, we'd see the last
shaft of sun those miners
ever saw there, naked,
thoughts of men who leap
from ledges, "You knew
Sanders died." "No."
as sad soldiers fall
from horses and lie
frozen in the snow.

The Royal Nonesuch

Extempore Effusion upon the Death
of Everette Maddox (1944–1989)

Given recent events,
it's easy to see why
that bilgewater-slick
New Orleans night
stink stays stuck
in the craw. Almost
midnight in The Maple
Leaf, and you, Big E.,
querulous for hours,
while black cascades
of rain made mighty sure
the never-ending steam-
bath just kept roaring.
Across Oak Street, through
the front bar window,
the red and blue KINKO'S
flickered and
flashed, reflecting
in the street like rubies
and sapphires. Then up
through the mildew, up
through the smoke, up off
that sticky Dixie Beer
floor, you raised it
at last, dog-eared
and dirty, on high
for me to read. And
I was so smitten, so
enamored, by
the incredible original
aptness of the title
of that somewhat-soiled
manuscript version
of your 2nd collection,

I exclaimed, "Damn!
I'll swap you one
fifth of Chivas for
the use of this!" And,
to my surprise, you
whispered, "OK." Given
recent events, I wish
I had offered a big
beef filet. But even
back then, you were, by
far, the absolutely
thinnest person I
had seen: only man
to match poem and
body to perfection:
paring things down
to the barest bone.
Given recent events,
and in verification
of your claim
that black
steambath night back
in 1983, something
a bit like sapphires
and rubies gleaming
in the streets, and
with, perhaps, just
a touch of a hint
of intent toward late
reparations, let me
say, sad pal, skinny
feller, funny friend,
and as the record runs
down now, you are, no

doubt about it, and
irrevocably so,
the one and the only,
the late Dauphin.

Felliniesque
1920–1993

In black and white a little boy runs down a beach pursued by priests.
Almost the young boy's earliest
recalled desire—
is to pee
in the padre's chalice,
or to spit
in the padre's sacristy wine,
or at least to sneak a drink
of Monsignor's best communion cabernet,
as acolytes are wont to do.
But no.

Soon enough the little boy runs through a house in black and white
full of Mama and nurses and so many aunts
and grandmama, and from whom
and where comes that distant
ethereal heavenly singing overhead?
Mama is bathing her little Guido,
swathing her lovely all in towels, warm
like swaddling, and ready to be
kissed and carried
upstairs to bed.
But no.

At last, the little boy runs down the beach by himself,
past salt marsh and seagrass,
the sea breeze flapping
his black Catholic cape
furiously behind
as he comes up short, stops
and stares
at the mascaraed mountain,
La Saraghina, the huge
disheveled goulash

of greasepaint, lipstick
and leers, sitting alone
in a chair
on the beach—
gazing forlornly out to sea.

The little boy holds out
coins in his hands, offers her
lire to dance the rhumba
while he sits
and watches, dance
the rhumba
while he sits and stares.
And O, she smiles
as he sees her rise,
turning toward him
to heave him her song.
All his life, the little boy
watches, those enormous haunches
steeped in the sea sand—
caught in that cadence
and stamp, he stares:
berouged Saraghina,
chiaroscuro—
calloused heels stomping
her ictus on sea sand. Bare feet pounding her rhythm on the shore.

Jaques Lured by Audrey

As the ox hath his bow . . .
—As You Like It

I swear I know not how, but as fleeting as
ice sculptures melting on a summer lawn,
opalescent in moonlight, winking like dark jade
out on the damp grass and away, these globes
of memory dissolve right down into the earth
as quick as all these goat droppings will in rain.
This very forest floor must be engorged by now
with generations of droppings, but no one sees
or cares. And how it happened I do not know, but
since that brief merger, since we pleasures proved,
O my adult arcade, my nut-brown study, my sylvan
nocturne in burnished beige and gold, it has been
like knocking at the deaf man's door of my brain
to thrust anything through there but that one moment,
this stopped dot of you growing more obscure each day,
your goat-reek rank on my hands like fresh garlic
and mint from the garden. How banish this dot
of you! Even though the thought itself is black
ink turning brown, this want will not burn down.
It flares in here, a never-flickering auto-da-fé,
an urge that will not purge, forever a hunger
nearly gnawing its way out. Banished now from
my own being, swaddled all in motley now, my
only wear—might we, together, be that beast
again, crushed mint, garlic, reek, balm, that ram,
O my tiny *Temptation of Saint Anthony,* together
might we make once more our common, curful cry.

Bottom's Dream

Methought I was—there is
no man can tell what.
            —A Midsummer Night's Dream

I'm the kind of guy who finds himself past midnight
halfway down the frigging kudzu-covered
woodbine-shaded moonlit emblematic forest path
self-conscious to a fault and wondering what
the hell these numerous assorted dead ends
are supposed to tally up to anyway.
                              "Jesus,
Jesus, Jesus," I have upon occasion in the dark
remarked, but don't think, by your leave,
I ever hung around expecting some response
to such direct address.
                    No.
I may be just the country cousin
forced sometime to city fair
to make a buck and to try my luck,
to tote and grunt, to cart
my baggage, hoist
my wares—my mildewed merchandise,
such as it is and so to speak—
but I ain't that dumb.
                    No
mother's son ever had to explain to me
that we are the zapped, the oblivion riders,
totally lacking—from the first time
that we mewl and cry—even a Chinaman's chance
of knowing the soiled shorts of a sick shyster
from a sack of sugar about the least damned thing.

Observe this bird, that bear, the wild herbs flowing down
yon fecund bank in damp and pearly moonshine.
As they are, so are we: tiny pitiful cogs
which scrape and grind the stars across the sky each night
only for all to dissolve at dawn.
                              And yet,

come morning I am still possessed by these brief
scenes, mists, vapors, frenzied residues.

                                But residues
of what? If man is but a bird, a bush, a bank
where the wild thyme blows; if, as to variations,
'tis all one between the ploughman, who comes and turns
the earth then lies beneath, and this bear
besmirching his face tonight with berries
only to besmear tomorrow his own buttocks with the same;
if all fall down in the great schemata,
why am I then left with these bad shreds of dreams,
these scraps of hair and hay,
these cobweb patches?
If I could get my hands back down beneath
the muck and stew, back down beneath
these floating fumes—
but such abiding wraiths, such furtive lingerers,
will not disperse. And all attempts become attempts
toward fathoming the unfathomable. Why
how exceedingly erectus, how very
pithecanthropine of me!

Swirling indistinct chimeras, I see them there
drifting up out of their own miasmal goo, from how
far down I think I'll never know, but if I perhaps
could offer to imbue them with the vestments
of this same locale—the vestments, say,
that I might wear me of a summer's day—
might they not then choose
to turn and to expound, having taken on
the accoutrements of said habitat, taking on
its language and its names as well?
And might we then converse us, our same raiments

engendering a commerce that we each could comprehend?
Or would these reveries, like great festering palms
swaying in their orchid fog, despite whatever garb
I might conceive, fold back into the dark quintessence
from which they came, continuing, forever, to exude
only the exotic, the entirely other, the secret idiom
lost in translation, distant, dim, inscrutable still?

Glendower Ponders the Vasty Deep

I can call spirits . . .
—Henry IV, Part I

If this wind in here would
         just lie down, these sounds
      like the clatter of cattle
            on a bridge
         could die down too.
      Is there a quick ocean somewhere,
   each ripple a labial
lapping the shore? There would I be.
   There would I dwell. For
      in here on the highways
            there's been a break in
         the action. In here,
      the Fords fly by, the conglomerates
      fume on the rank horizon,
the sun goeth down. Amen to the sun.
            Amen to the coil
         and climb of days come down. Long
   gone is the horse I rode
in on. It is not like you
      cannot see yourself, fists
            in the air, Fords flying
   by, not like you
do not hear yourself, hear
      a voice that could be
   only you, though distant and wrong,
         saying, "Just kneel down
         and kiss the water, Jack. That
will bring back the tide." No,
   not much like there was ever
      a way, or a word,
      or a name to cry out but
         to call forth, demand that
   some entity, somewhere, ignite here,
      here at the edge

of a dead sea, at the hind tit
of time, the oil, I pray,
of an anointing. If this wind
in here would just die down.

Reynaldo in Paris

"Ooo-la-la!" remarked Reynaldo. "Tonight
my wick shall dip in ecstasies once more
as I plunge deeper through that nunnery door,
Miss Mimi's house of sale, then jam it tight.
Back home, I smelled the rotten fault all right,
so took the bucks and split from that dumb bore
and got out while the gettin' was good, before
shit hit the fan and blotted out the light.

What wine so sweet as little Mimi's seat!
Now that's the song I'm singing every day.
So let them grab each other by the balls.
For what care I whose slick, incestuous meat
gets gnawed between those sheets. And, what care they
for fardel-bearing sots who play their thralls."

Pro Quo

Higgledy-piggledy
Sergei M. Eisenstein
Needed State financing:
Film is not free.

"Only," said Stalin, "if
Revisionistically
Ivan the Terrible
Acts just like me."

Fortuna's Fool

Higgledy-piggledy
Romeo Montague
Copped a quick feel at a
Party one night—

Started events ending
Contralascivious,
Deadly, disgusting, no
Cocksman's delight.

Morte D'Arthur

Higgledy-piggledy
Alfred, Lord Tennyson
Lost his pal Hallam to
Fever and flu:

"One hundred thirty-one
Ultramemorial
Verses and, man, I still
Can't bury you."

I Greet You

Higgledy-piggledy
Ralph Waldo Emerson
Often wrote poems that
Lay down and died.

Walt Whitman sent him his
Preponderatingly
Better book. Emerson
Read it, and cried.

Room with a View

Higgledy-piggledy
Emily Dickinson
Looked out her front window
Struggling for breath,

Suffering slightly from
Agoraphobia:
"Think I'll just stay in and
Write about Death."

Primer Litter

Higgledy-piggledy
"Old Possom" Eliot
Wrote childish verse about
Practical cats.

"These are for all of you
Abecedarians,
Idiots, simpletons,
Moronic brats."

Homework

Higgledy-piggledy
Erin Elizabeth
Stokesbury said, "Math is
Too hard for me."

O for those summers of
Unalgebraical
$13 + 2 -$
$12 - 3.$

Old Times There

Higgledy-piggledy
"Red" Robert Penn Warren
Moved way up North from his
Home in the South—

Looked over Yale and with
Cynosurality
Made them all swallow him:
Grits in the mouth.

Dark Blurb of the Soul

". . . Seems to me to be
   one of that breed who, when
he approaches Dallas from
   the north, sees, welling
up, gold chunks of buildings,
   great glass in the sun, row
over row of gold teeth, hog
   grins, glistening, blind.
Here we have the mnemonic
   daring, the nasty clarity,
the handprint of necessity
   of one of those 'intellectuals'
attempting the flamenco
   over a Big Abyss. This
is the kind of bore who views
   the abominable Hawaiian
photo of Mom and Uncle
   Joe, loud shirts, volcano
in the background, and then
   lets the sad sow metaphors
multiply and cry. This is
   he, this is he who sees
the burned girl, that fried
   face's texture like plastic
puke, and aches to get his
   hands on all that saffron
and blue. Reading this entity
   is stepping off into
slime, into little fishes, fast
   and crappy creatures nipping
at your knees. Subtleties
   of rhythm? Subtleties of
rhyme? If swine had wings,
   this guy would fly . . ."

For My Daughter

I often swore that I had never raised an arm,
but then I would recall
that night you could not quite
comprehend fractions: if sixteen pints
occupied two-thirds of one container
how many pints would be required to fill
another that was one-fourth full
with the same number of pints poured in:
and I recall the slap of the back of the hand
of the tone of my voice drenched
with impatience, how it slammed you, blam
against the wall, your eyes confused,
confused like the day you came back
a half hour late from somewhere
with your little friend, and I screamed
declaring you *stupid,* right
on the button, and as you lay there
gasping, my realizing only then
the extra lick, that kick
to the gut of calling you *stupid*
in front of your little friend:
pages of illustrations: no different
really from the day seven years ago—
you were four and had wandered off
in the supermarket, looking at all
the various meats, the various vegetables,
chickens and beef and zucchini
in their glory, when I had told you to stay
right by my side, so I hid from you
on purpose, to teach you a lesson,
and when you could not find me and thought
I had abandoned you, and ran about
confused, tears streaming down that loveliness,
and then I revealed myself, all

transfiguration emerging from the breakfast foods,
and how you ran to me
in your ecstasy, what a zinger twang
to the solar plexus, what a line drive
to the old breadbasket, a sucker punch,
what an eight-ounce-glove shot straight
like a shiv to the ribs, sprinting to embrace
the very thing that caused your pain—
pages of illustrations:
and if it is true, and it is,
that I sometimes look in your eyes
and believe you to be
the most beautiful being,
and if it is true that I have acted
on many occasions in accordance with such love,
there still remain these moments
where I see now there was never any reason,
any justification, for such actions,
except my own fragility—
then allow me to state
that I see what I have done,
that I would not do it longer, that I would
offer up here, in this semi-public forum, a construct
or creation, containing this affidavit, this
testimonial entry, maxima culpa, this rendering,
dearest, this account, this expiation.

The Legacy

for Erin

Just so, when they come demanding,
you might possess some grasp of facts—
just in case motivations at some point
might appear unclear—just
to insure with certainty

you will recall later on: take
one peeled cucumber now and grate it
finely as you can. Swirl this and the juice
of two lemons with one pint
of yogurt, setting it

aside somewhere, cold. So
there will remain some record, cube
three pounds of lamb, then sauté it
lightly floured, in a skillet
with one stick of butter, dice

one large onion, then combine
the meat and onion in a stew pot
under water enough to cover all. To this
mixture add three bay leaves, add
three cloves of garlic

crushed. Add one tablespoon
of pepper, then one teaspoon of salt. In-
to that you sprinkle cumin: three
teaspoonsful, and then to make
it strange, two heaping

teaspoonsful of powdered
cardamom, a grayish beige in its dry
state (but it will turn the water green),
and then you cover this and cook it
for three hours on low heat: stir

the soup occasionally, but
do not let the liquor boil away. Remember:
when they come in the night, screaming
with their torches, beseeching
you, fingers of torchlight

warping their wan faces
in that dark, your front porch flickering
unearthly, remember then what
I say now: after the lamb
has simmered for three hours,

in a separate saucepan
cook two cups of rice. While the rice
is cooking, peel, then slice in white
inch-thick circles, three large
eggplants. Fry each slice

in extra light olive oil
in a skillet until browned and heavy, then
place the eggplant out on paper
towels to soak some oil away—
(by now the cardamom

has drenched your house
in incense: massive hints of orient,
odalisque, Babylon and Berber,
Bedouin and myrhh) just
so I will know you

know, layer in a casserole
first the lamb, then the eggplant, then
rice on top of that: lamb again, egg-
plant, rice, until the dish
is almost full—then

                    pour the chartreuse
juice into the casserole: bake it covered
for an hour, in an oven, at three hundred
            eighty-five degrees—but whatever
                    else, do not forget

                    they will be coming, certain
as the glacier's pain, wrapped in cowls,
in their injunctions, screws and ropes,
            racks, chains, insisting
                    you confess

                    your sickness, producing writs
commanding you disclose what sources
taught you to concoct such venom,
            declaring all your actions
                        darkness, everything you live for

                    bane. Child, do not listen,
do not answer. Deny them. Lie to them
at every path (a thick, green, good,
            sweet pungency for hours
                    will have lacquered

                    every wall, satiated, smeared
the air, redolent, ancient, tang
of loam or salt or sea) but remember:
            when the dish comes from the oven
                    you must serve it

                    right away. In the middle
of a large, hot, black plate, stack
a steaming mountain of the lamb—
            then along its peak, pile
                    three dollops of the lemon-

yogurt mixture—snows
melting from the heat, cascading off
the mountainside in tiny milky rivulets,
   the smallest runny tributaries
      winding out to sea. And

   at this point in time, when
the heat and cold conjoin, you must
call forth your beloved. You must sit
   your beloved down. You must ask
      of your beloved

   if he wants for any thing.
Then place there, before him, the plate
you have prepared; permit him to sample
   (always know they will be coming;
      they carry metal rams to batter

   in your door) your creation:
daughter, when he lifts it to his tongue—
O, at that precise moment, daughter,
   from all previous moorings
      his heart will be set free.

Lauds

Even in Texas there's a rose on the air
for that quick half-hour during summer dawn.
And we, *new meat,* the summer "college boys,"
began our first good look at things
that thirty minutes before time
when the *permanents* came in
to the Texas State Highway Department barn
to sip the liquor of a cup of coffee—
and then go.

Rysinger would not shut up.
No one could shut him up.
Rysinger was our fathers' age,
and every day brought his constant routine,
each morning commencing as a string of jokes
dirtier than the day before. Each day:
if he could gargle forth some image, some
froth,
so strange to the *new meat*
that it could make us turn our eyes away—
then that would make him grin and giggle.
Each day.

But now when I think of Rysinger,
I do not think first of that morning
Plaunty came back from his honeymoon
and Rysinger followed him around asking:
Plaunty?
Why is your mouth all puckered up?
What you been eating, Plaunty,
to cause your mouth to pucker so? Lemons?
Lemons, Plaunty?
And neither do I think of Rysinger's story
of getting two milkshakes down at Dick's Drive-In, nor

of his particularly energetic rendition of The Tale
of Granddaddy's French Ticklers, which
brought old Grandma back to life, which
made her go "Whoa!" and then
"Oh!" and then
"Soooooieeeee!"

What I always remember about Rysinger
is the two or three times that summer
along about three or four in the afternoon
when the heat on some country road was killing us,
and the hot asphalt would steam up in our faces,
would billow and speckle our clothes and faces,
and there was nothing but heat,
the world being endless waves of heat—
and I would look over and see Rysinger
trying to hide his red eyes,
making gestures that tried to imply
it was the steam, or the wind,
or the sweat in his eyes,
that made them burn,
there,
by the side of the road.

City Lights

Today on the north beltway
in my rear-view mirror

a powder beige Mercedes
grazed a big black car

then rolled over twice
in air, before bouncing down

sideways, to be slammed
by a trailer truck into

the retaining wall. All
this comes

rerunning
in sepias,

and silent, like
that brief, grainy

four seconds of film
where two locomotives

collide, and when they
collide, the smoke

billows up silent, and
gears and wheels eject

from the engines
silent, no sound,

as quiet as a thin
pale, slip

of a fish,
disturbed

and jerking away
from first light

at the dark,
formless bottom

of the sea.— I
was one-half mile farther

through the afternoon,
the late sun suffusing

everything, concrete
and sky, to a watered-down

mescal, when it even
occurred some action

of mine might be
required. Surely

ambulances, mystical,
imposing crimson

blinks and clangs, were
already setting out

like pulsing antibodies
to cleanse the scene.

It is this way
with things—

back home tonight,
I celebrate

my return with a somewhat
larger Canadian Club

which, after that first
deep bee sting, neat

on the back of the tongue,
really is vaguely

like velvet. Through
my 2nd story complex

window, the mercury arc-
lights bathe my face

orchid, and bathe each
oleander, oak and sidewalk

beneath them as lovely
a shade of lavender

as any beginning abrasion
or Wal-Mart parking lot.

There are so many
electric wires on poles

now, crisscrossing
the dark, but one

black wire connects me
directly to the All-Star

Wrestling Arena's static
and roar. While outside

the pale maniacal moths
continue their kamikaze

orbits and dives
around streetlights

and char. I know
soon I will shut off

the main event, draw
the curtains, lie down

in my bed and listen
to the thuds in the central

air. But when I close
my eyes, what I see

is that blur of beige on
the beltway, over and over,

receding into the rear-
view mirror, my god my

god my god, smaller and
smaller into the filthy

sunset, totally
aimless, devoid

of sound, burning
away into the rush-

hour fumes.—It
is this way now:

each of us sent to bed
without supper, sweat

and white brightness
blinding out all

beyond ringside,
drunk insects drifting

up into the tic and hum
and heat of the vapor

lamps. Then, lumbering
forward, the masked,

muscled, Umbrageous
Other—standing and

stomping, mouthing
every label and brand

name known. What
does it mean? Grinding

the grit in his teeth,
scratching his hot-red

Day-Glo crotch, while
we, in one last crack

of an instant, reach
our hands upward and

out to drown down
into darkness, silent—

the slightest
things fleeing

from light
along the deep

cold ocean
floor—only

to realize
his hands

are raised too—
holding a gray

metal folding chair
over his head.

Autumn Rhythm

. . . energy and motion made visible . . .
—Jackson Pollock

These are not trees. These black
dollops and drips and plops are not
the bare limbs of Mooresses gliding
through twilight in Central Park,
are not sycamores giving off
a reek sweet as squashed possum
rotting in a roadside ditch,
are nothing like the bent bars
of Rikers nor bare ruined choirs
nor the dry, crushed stubble
of a frozen field. The white
is not snow, is not clouds seen
through bleak sticks, nor soiled
strips of Kotex flung among twigs.
And yet. And yet discerned from
a distance, I can see how some
Nebraskan, some matriarch
maybe from one of those families
rich enough to keep a dwarf
around, might squint, frown,
then begin to conceive of this
pane of beige as a background
for a landscape of the fall.
Maybe. But to me it fades
as close to the colors of old
watered-down scotch as anything.
If anything. The impulsive
result of a nameless need
if anything. A penumbral
whirling dervish version
of Dizzy Gillespie maybe.
Jesus, Jesus, who can say?
No, never lariat loops or
swoops, or bird droppings

in bruised wine, as some ass
once said. No oil of tears.
Never, probably, any dark
intermingling of asterisks
or octopi. Not much
at all, I don't believe,
like the lastest product from
the casket factory, laid
down here in a pane of beige
to be slung upon, and then
dribbled on as a background
for a landscape of the fall.

The Pear

Rysinger sits, and skins the pear
carefully. The knife goes round,
and soon the damp white flesh is seen.

The green thin peelings fall at last
in ringlets on the floor. And now
he holds the fruit in hand, a glistening moon.

Rysinger sits, and eats the pear
with speed. For—if one thing
he has learned—

                    he's learned
the whiteness soon turns brown.

Ready to Satisfy All Your Bereavement Needs

The preacher who delivered the eulogy
at Wardell's Funeral Home
in Oklahoma City
churned on and on—
ladling out what he perceived
to be the virtuous cream
of my father's bounty
far and away.
                    But
I cannot recall today
what it was precisely
the preacher who delivered the eulogy
at my father's funeral said—
because at that particular time
I found it impossible
to concentrate on what
the preacher had to say—
because just as the preacher
who delivered the eulogy
began, I got the most
wonderful idea for a poem.

This Print of Dürer's

In this print of Dürer's hanging on the wall
The knight and horse are old but very strong.
The lines run down his face, his body clothed
Completely in thick armor that he loves.
His friend, a dog, runs gladly at his heel,
And they'll crush skulls before the day is gone.
Behind him loom monsters and monstrosities
That he's absorbed, or beaten, either way.

And Death arrives. His face sits on his sleeve,
An hourglass in his hand. The knight—
Is not afraid. No doubt he knows his way.
And there, see, on a hill, the furthest thing
Away, already passed, but visible, stand
The towers of a town where peace might be.

Little Keats Soliloquy

You're probably wondering
what I'm doing with this
2-by-4 said a stableboy,
and when I came to with
dried blood in my ear
I knew that I had
missed the joke again.
It happens all the time:
that was no refried banana
that was my wife. That
means something? Meant nothing
to me while they grinned
their asses off. You go
straight to hell I said;
but I can't go through
life this way, always outside
watching the baker
plopping pastries into
sacks for other kids,
that's no good, I know
that for sure, but what
can I do, what can I
use for a ladder, what
to carry me up into
the loft, away from these
stinking horses?

Often in Different Landscapes

What should be done? No one knew for sure.
"Look at that chili-dog," I said to the blind guy,
after which I took it on the lam. The entire
offended countryside was up in arms. *The Scourge
of Sheboygan* the media labeled me. Those swine,
they forced me to the forests, taking shelter
in an abandoned hunting lodge. And only sometimes,
on the weekends, would I hear the snickering sounds
of couples in the woods. That first night, that
lonely night, the sleep dripped from my eyes,
was replaced by more, and rain dripped, and the dark
with its hard tonnage, I should add, also dripped,
oozing like hot asphalt under the door. Why
did it remind me so much of the blind guy
and his constant drool? My gorge rose. But not
for long. I packed those days with simple things,
taking up the Ace comb with cellophane, playing
songs of my own invention, such as "Johnny Belinda
Where Is Thy Sting," a personal favorite. But that, too,
sometimes brought thoughts of the blind guy, why
I don't know. And neither do I understand
where these recurring images come from, strange
images, often in different landscapes, and always
coming back, huge indigestions, to glut
my sleep, my waking moments, all my life
clogged with glossolalia, white canes, shrieks, slobber,
the spastic I tripped once behind the gym.

The Murder of Gonzago and His Friends

In a district that's rarely traveled these days,
in a place where even the blackbirds lie down
in daylight, just north of West Fork,
I fell out with eight debauchees below some sycamores.
"Good fellows, arise!" I cried. "I
suspect you have heard the sad news."
But they were dull, sluggard, adamant, insane.
And besides, Mogen David seemed their chief concern.
The Arapahoes would soon be upon us: "Arise! Arise!
Shall blood-purple be the color of our pain?"
Nothing. Their eyes were not white rapids.
But no one could say I did not try. No one felt
I was to blame. No one. This was many years ago.
At night now, when I leave the house
with my jar of salt, my thoughts are of them. Each night
as I stand under my streetlight, I can think
only of them. And as I look down the long row
of streetlights, each with its own person,
holding his own jar, as I stand there
pouring salt on the slugs, that then blister and foam,
as I watch them dissolve, my thoughts are always of them.

What It Feels Like to Live in This Country to Me

Where are all those yucks? With a more silent nature
than that of the corpse's fingernail stretching out
on the silk, up from the sea of stone, the sea
from which thought does not arise, an emotion
is headed our way. And speaking of fingernails,
I saw a movie once where they buried this guy
alive, because they thought he was dead. He wasn't. Later on,
they dug him up and he was. Fingernails, stubs, had raked
that coffin lid until it was streaked, smeared. He
wanted out, see. What could be more plain? Ah, now,
the guiding light is followed by the edge of night,
has been for years, and this experience, myself,
me and the television I'm observing at this
very minute, Bob Hope, with the sound off, bid a fond
farewell, to paraphrase Rilke somewhat loosely,
from the ballroom of the ambiguously blessed, and
O those cards and O those letters, communication,
reason is where it's at, but, as I said
with considerable power, in another poem
of my own making, Where is it?, who knows,
and to be quite honest, who gives a shit, what did I
just say?, Huntz Hall be with me till I end my song,
the log has been flogged behind the gray barn now,
out there, where snow is embraced gently by the earth,
where the earth is soaked from all that embracing, where
there is only a speck left, that's where it's at
after all, yes sir, just a dot, a raft at sea,
undefined, no distinguishing marks, the last placebo,
fading away like a stain into the realms of rue.

Footlight Parade

A short man was excited. He wanted to put on
a show. Women were dancing. He was excited.
People ran around. A blonde woman liked him. But
he didn't know it. He liked another woman.
Well, he got drunk. He wasn't supposed to though.
Women were dancing. They were singing. Then, the blonde
woman saved him. He talked fast. He was excited.
Some other things happened. He put on the show.
Another man and woman sang in it. She was
so pretty. They were in a big hotel. It was called
Honeymoon Hotel. They sang in the hotel. They sang
in the halls. More people came and sang. The man
and woman went to bed and sang. That was the end
of that show. Well, then the man who sang asked
the woman who sang to marry him. She said she would.
He kissed her. Then they put on another show. The man
and woman sang again. Then a lot of women swam.
They were happy. They swam. They were pretty. Then
that was the end of that show. Then they went
and put on another show. The first man got in a fight.
Then *he* danced and sang. He was a sailor then.
After that show was over, he asked the blonde woman
to marry him. She smiled. She said she would.

California

Shouldn't we finally get going.
I mean I think the right time has come.
The wind drops the leaves to the ground.
I think we had better get going.
The sunrise, the sunrise has fallen.
The long rows of waves keep on coming.
They lap in the rocks by the shore.

I mean it is dusk on the shore.
And the wind kicks the leaves to the ground.
All over the black leaves are falling.
Why do we still only stand here?
The time for our starting has come.
Let us go to the boats and launch out.
I think it would be best to run.

What I mean is the sunrise is gone.
Let us run to the boats and start rowing.
The leaves, the leaves keep on falling.
The black leaves have covered the beaches.
And why do we still only stand here?
I mean why do we still only stand here?

What the New Chef Said

"Those tapioca-type idiots
who come in here expecting
some kind of lethargic lull
to fill their puffed-out paunches
had damn better lift
their lardy asses up
and right on out the door. If
they hang long around here
I'll take a skewer
and stick the hogs, rotten
or not. What they want
is the old way, the old slow
metronome of flavors chopped
out and dropped on a plate
to set before the dunce.
That's over! All over!
Today's green salads
are the truly tossed
with sundry graffiti of zucchini
and weenie and bologna sprinkled
over all. I give the people
what the world is really like:
strawberry buttermilk
and prune pie. Ice
creams lost in sauerkraut.
That sweet-and-sour sauce
is what I make and
what I make is what (though
it bust their ulcerous guts)
what they devour!" he said.

To Laura Phelan: 1880–1906

for James Whitehead

Drunk I have been. And drunk I was that night
I lugged your stone across the other graves,
to set you up a hundred yards away.
Flowers I found, then. Drunk I have been.
And am, standing here with no moon to spill
on the letters of your name; my loud fingers
feeling them out. The stone is mossed over
And why must I bring myself in the dark
to stand here among the sour grasses
that stain my white jeans? Drunk I have been.
See, the thick dew slides on the trees, wet weeds,
wetness smears the air; and a vague surf
of wildflowers pushes my feet, slipping
close to my legs. When the thought comes at last
that people fall apart, that the things we do
will not do. Ends. Then, we come to scenes
like this. This scene of you. You apart:
this is not you; and yet, this is where I stand
and close my eyes, and feel the ragged wind
blow red and maul my hair. In the night somewhere,
dandelions foam. This is not you. Drunk
I have been. Across this graveyard, that
is where you are. Yet I stand here. Would ask
things of your name. Would wish. Would not be told
of the stink in the skull, the eye's collapse.
Would be told something new, something unknown.—
A mosquito bites my hand. The only sound
is the rough wind. Drunk I have been,
here, at the loam's maw, before this stone
of yours, which is not you. Which is.

Song of the Incredible Lonzo

Thick hours lie like braces and the tang
of quite a few daiquiris collects around
the yellow bottoms of the tongues of Sue
and Shirley yanking fishsticks from the stove O
and ah my sweet Jesus is it not at this time
in the cool of the evening in the cool
of the day usually an old girl's fancy
turns to thoughts now of the incredible Lonzo
crawling over the backyard fence or maybe
up the drain or coming God from somewhere
importantly unexpected but never the clothes hamper
with its white shirts' ballpoint pens left in
in darkness as now on comes Lonzo the fair
the magnificent Lonzo that wild one she cries
salty sweat making muscles glisten in
the sun the sweet salad of his hair blowing
she cries O and again O and Lonzo my
beloved may might must can could the quick
brown fox this this at last is given unto me
as into the room roar those strangers her
own children her fine children her very own
white rabbits of the night demanding mayonnaise

But Once in Special

Get out of here with your ideas about
going downtown to see that roller coaster
and no I do not want to buy any more
ping pong balls now look this is my room
I pay the rent so please remove
these midgets and try to understand
it's nothing personal actually I've
always liked shorter Get away from that
aquarium if you don't mind God damn
people this is well OK see it was
the other day or maybe last year
I don't remember too clearly anymore
I slid into this out of sight witch
her dark eyes sadder than the sea
try to understand when she moved the air
flowed out in waves before her and she moved
so softly those waves they still keep rolling over me

Gifts

They say that blood is salt. I've
tasted yours, and they are right.
So let's get on with our big painting
exchange. In mine, I've placed you
in a black pasture, with black horses,
your red eyes clearly discerned. But,
and I observe you're having the same
problem, here in the middle distance
isn't really the right place for you
somehow. Over more to the left,
I think, yes, under that smeared vision
of crows, way out in those dark, waist-high
weeds, there, leaning against that
huge pile of horseshit, yes, and a little
nearer the vanishing point, thank you.

Religious Poem

A Shakespearean dusk in November.
Bleak scenes. Bone trees, and so on.
Let my many gargoyle faces come whirling!
Oh, which to choose. Shall it be Paul Scofield
as Sir Thomas More? Jesus no! Or how about
Jesus? That's one I've done. Of course I
never admitted it was Jesus; and often I
would change the appearance, so it looked like
someone besides Jesus. After all, if
people saw a person going around with
the face of Jesus on, well, that would be
a little self-indulgent. I mean, Jesus
is a deity and everything; some people
might see it as a sacrilege. Anyone might.
You have to be real careful. I
argued with myself, and so on, and on.

On the Comeback Trail

The sad-eyed riders of the purple sage
are burning ranches out along
the foggy distant northern borders.
It was they who took the complete works
of Winslow Homer off into the hills.
They burned them. Lord, the flakes and pigments
fell for days from those mile-high haciendas.
Word came that several halfway houses
were smoulders too. And so. That settled it.
Leaving behind even Miss Eikenhorst, bright braces
glinting up her smiles; leaving behind
an unspoken, alas, passion for said fine freshman
remedial English student; leaving
dumplings behind, this dude:
me: myself: I: simply just left town.
The rest of this poem will be in the first person.
I don't know how I did it. The way
was long. With Mortimer Ennis, my faithful
Indian companion, I strove. But even he
fell away, tempted by weirdnesses
at the outer provinces. How in the hard times
the weak do wash away! Strange. At last,
to have reached these windows. And now. Now
simply step out. "Simply" was the word all along.
There. Done. So. Isn't that a song playing somewhere?
I think. . . . Yes. It is. It is "Never No More
Blues." Wait. Wait. No, it is "Moonlight and Skies."

Why I Find Myself Immersed in Few Traditions

So what if the world needed potatoes.
Columbus could have lied when he went back.
Too easily satisfied, those chocolate eyes
of the native girls were slanted enough for him.
It isn't his fault really. How could he have
foreseen these orange arroyos where the people
come to dream of sleep? I'm here right now,
and I can barely believe it myself:
the hot nights, the brown trees making
the insane clicking sounds of a hundred cicadas,
these numerous dry and vaguely heart-shaped rocks.
Now so what if an after-dinner smoke
is nice. What's that when you can't tell
the moon from the streetlights. And even when you can
it looks covered with lint. Oh sure, we and everything
keep going on and on. But let me tell you,
when our caryatids start crumbling,
and when we wait in our western airports
longing for tickets to non-existent lands,
our luggage heavy with a few big books,
then, buddy, it makes it pretty damned hard
to lean on the past, when you see all this
as just the final end of a lot of peristalsis.

The Zany

Once upon a time we were all sitting around in the tomb
after supper when this guy comes to the door
dressed in the skin of one of those animals
that swore they would never die and introduced himself
as certainly The New Midas For Our Times
and so he says to us he says

watch me

Glory he made the prongs of a pitchfork glow
Glory he fried an egg in his palm
Glory he touched books and the books burned
and then he finished
by reaching for the one he said he loved

Tears would pool
then sizzle down each flushed cheek and away

Wow

I was impressed

My name
by the way
is The Wild Bull Of The Pampas

Here comes
The Wild Bull Of The Pampas
people often say

Beautiful

But now I feel I know
what The New Midas meant when

he spoke of a weariness
at hearing
each time
the titty pink applause
of various groups
who screamed Lawzee
and such

somehow

There was this traveling salesman
see who stopped for the night
at the home of this farmer
who had two really fine daughters
and a prize milk cow oh yeah

But that isn't what I wanted to say

And neither was that

and so forth

and so on

These birds in the trees
these leaves in the trees
these pale flowers in the grass I mow
these remind me now
of cosmologies not my own

and the arms tire

and the heart tires

And the song slows down
to the wrong speed

Which reminds me
of this jukebox
see in Burkeville Texas
which would play
if you punched c-6
a record supplied by the Ku Klux Klan
which went
Move them niggers north boys
Move them niggers north
If they don't like our southern ways
Move them niggers north oh yeah

No

That isn't it

That isn't what I wanted to say

somehow

And neither was that

And so on

I think
I wanted to say something
about when the odors of leaves
would return to these voices
about when I could talk about
the children again

about when I can walk there
in the high grass
where the beast grazes
at ease
with a quiet strength
waiting to engender
and join a slow
a soft falling into

the pool

of the peace

of this earth

yeah

that
is a little like
something I wanted to say

The Lamar Tech Football Team Has Won Its Game

The Lamar Tech football team has won its game.
My grandmother has died. The newspaper, yesterday,
Said, "Siamese Twins Cut Apart, One Lives." My father
Says, "Some things you have to learn to accept
Take the good parts with the bad."
                              (This must be a dream.)
"Oh, yes," I say. "I remember how the sun feels warm
Even on the coldest days, sometimes."
The Lamar Tech football team.   The newspaper.

Belgium is now importing jukeboxes.
Australians are installing oil heaters.
Adversity is what makes you mature. "Oh, yes.
"I've seen the winter moon pumped up, platinum-like;
And the stars seem brightest when it's freezing."
Siamese twins.   On the coldest days, sometimes.
                              (This must be a dream.)
My father says, "Make hay while the sun shines."
The sun.   The moon.   Belgium is now importing
Jukeboxes.   One lives.   My father says, "In a few weeks
You'll feel better. Time is a great healer."   The sun.
The moon.
The Lamar Tech football team has won its game.

East Texas

The taste in my mouth
Was the taste of blood or rust on backdoor thermometers
Unread for twenty years. With my cheesecloth
Net I waited in the woods. Then the flutters
Of the giant swallowtails could be heard far away. Leaves
Moved. Sweat was acid in my eyes, and my father frowned
In his huge wheelchair. He could not get up the hill. My last two loves
Sat in pine straw, waiting to see what I would do. The sound
To my left was the sound of men standing at urinals.
But no. It was only the rain, uncontrollable, and the rain took
The gray shapes of steam. My father frowned. It was so steep.
And those shapes were the shapes of old women with shawls
On their heads, of old men sitting down. She shook
Me saying I was talking in my sleep.

To All Those Considering Coming to Fayetteville

Often these days, when my mind holds splinters
like the pieces of the Old Spice bottle
I dropped and shattered yesterday, I think
of other places. It is wintertime now,
and the Ozarks are hushed up with snow
everywhere. They are small mountains, almost
not mountains at all, but rather, with trees
sticking up, they seem more like
the white hairy bellies of fat old men
who have lain down here. What has this to do
with anything? I don't know. Except
it makes me think of snow elsewhere, and what
it would be like to be there. I might drive
across Oklahoma, then on into
New Mexico. I could be there tonight.
The land would be flat, the snow over
everything. The highway straight, and forever
the snow like blue cheese in the moonlight,
for as far as there is, and air, cold air
crisp as lettuce, wet lettuce in the store,
and I would keep driving, on and on.

Summer in Fairbanks

is like a dull dream. From time to time
the paperboy comes grinning with proof that
something has happened after all. Here
where the highways end. To go north
from here, you must be a bird or wealthy.
The prospectors have each been starved and strained
away down southward and to old folks homes.
Here is where the nights end too. Never
to sense the dark for days is strange, and not
so hot as one might think. It is strange
always to be able to see, and say:
that is there and that is there and that
is over there, always. Strange, not to tell
the end of days by any other way
than clocks, and meals; televisions turning off.
Different, for things to seem
to the eyes like one day, that somehow
has slowed down to months, years, icebergs
of minutes so separated by an absence
from anything that ever came before,
that the anxious people find themselves
waiting for the swish on their lime lawns
of the dirty tennis shoes of
the grinning paperboy who brings them yesterday.

The North Slope

Three months away from the word away from trees
and bushes hills newspapers women dark
on into the undeodorized the raw
twelve hours a day seven days a week
helicopters dropped us on tundra unrelieved
abandoned well sites to do away with
anything "environmentally unsound" there that
first day stacking scrap metal thinking the last words
of Scarlett O'Hara seeing how flat
the land was how brown how completely
unrelieved the flatness how raw the air
coming off the Arctic sea the horizon
a pencil line sometimes blending
with the frigid summer sky unrelieved
a foot and a half of tundra and under it
ice going down frozen earth eighteen hundred feet
I remember the small tundra flowers
delicate white blue the yellow poppies
in the second week I reached out to pick some
saw a jut of ice beside them
reaching up strange I shivered strange
something there I did not quite understand
could not get my mind around something
ice underneath them then back at base camp
before bed thought again and again
coldness what is it I thought strange unrelieved
more and more could not look at the flat
horizon or would not would keep my gaze away
from the white sky white fog the white
light from the sun never sinking what is it
I did not know only this feeling
someone walking always away something unsaid
and I kept my head down away from the sun the sky
then came the week of the caribou
the herds they came running unrelieved
thousands and thousands across the tundra
I kept my head down but at last could not

a hundred yards away two wolves loping behind
I saw them drag down a slow one
it was one hundred yards away
I saw them could not believe saw them
the red meadow of its side this was
one hundred yards away watched them eat
there was ice underground is ice
underground could not believe saw them rip ice
from its side ice the color of the sun I saw
it was raw it was nothing that fell from
its side ice emptiness came loping as birds
so many birds flew away and away screaming over
something they seemed to have heard
unrelieved the sound now of blood falling
of ice now and of whaleboats I could not believe
thinking her last words what was it the birds said
going away what was it the ice whispered raw
could not lift my head
the jet trails sagged over Dead Horse
and drifted away here where you aim
the harpoon sailor see it surface see it wallow
unrelieved see it dive here where the wait is
the ache for anything anything not dropping away
she breaches she breaches they cried and that
image charging my head all that white reaching
up that vacuum revealed unrelieved
and the froth all the spray and it sinking back
under leaving me asking for some other thing
for some other way asking time
to turn to forget what is there what is not
everywhere birds kept flying away
but Scarlett Scarlett this is the place
where tomorrow never comes the sun like
red ice searing always the summer the land
of absence of nothing of cold of no night
the wind blowing frozen off the Arctic sea

The Polar Bear

In the only land where things are truly white,
The polar bear is too.
                          He lumbers about,
His round, white stomach full of fish.
The meat of the fish lies white inside him;
His thick, shaggy coat shines white in the sun.
And as he moves of snow and ice,
He slips out of sight before our eyes
In an almost magical blending of light.

And the polar bear has this land to himself.
All to himself he roams the ice;
For very few creatures, and fewer men,
Can live with the always unbending of white.

Like no man I know of, he sleeps at night
With his stomach, and dreams, full of white.

To His Book

Wafer; thin and hard and bitter pill I
    Take from time to time; pillow I have lain
        Too long on; holding the brief dreams, the styled
Dreams, the nightmares, shadows, red flames high
    High up on mountains; wilted zinnias, rain
        On dust, and great weight, the dead dog, and wild
Onions; mastodonic woman who knows how,—
    I'm tired of you, tired of your insane
        Acid eating in the brain. Sharp stones, piled
Particularly, I let you go. Sink, or float, or fly now,
               Bad child.

III

Unsent Message to My Brother in His Pain

Please do not die now. Listen.
Yesterday, storm clouds rolled
out of the west like thick muscles.
Lightning bloomed. Such a sideshow
of colors. You should have seen it.
A woman watched with me, then we slept.
Then, when I woke first, I saw
in her face that rest is possible.
The sky, it suddenly seems
important to tell you, the sky
was pink as a shell. Listen
to me. People orbit the moon now.
They must look like flies around
Fatty Arbuckle's head, that new
and that strange. My fellow American,
I bought a French cookbook. In it
are hundreds and hundreds of recipes.
If you come to see me, I shit you not,
we will cook with wine. Listen
to me. Listen to me, my brother,
please don't go. Take a later flight,
a later train. Another look around.

Day Begins at Governor's Square Mall

Here, newness is all. Or almost all. And like
a platterful of pope's noses at a White House dinner,
I exist apart. But these trees now—
how do you suppose they grow this high in here?
They look a little like the trees I sat beneath in 1959
waiting with my cheesecloth net for butterflies.
It was August and it was hot. Late summer,
yes, but already the leaves in trees were
flecked with ochers and the umbers of the dead.
I sweated there for hours, so driven,
so immersed in the forest's shimmering life,
that I could will my anxious self not move
for half a day—just on the imagined chance
of making some slight part of it my own.
Then they came. One perfect pair of just-hatched
black-and-white striped butterflies. The white
lemon-tipped with light, in shade
then out, meandering. Zebra swallowtails,
floating, drunk in the sun, so rare to find
their narrow, fragile, two-inch tails intact.
At that moment I could only drop my net and stare.
The last of August. 1959. But these trees, now,
climb up through air and concrete never hot or cold.
And I suspect the last lepidoptera that found
themselves in here were sprayed then swept away.
Everyone is waiting though, as before a storm—
anticipating something. Do these leaves never fall?

Now, and with a mild surprise, faint
music falls. But no shop breaks open yet.
The people, like myself, range aimlessly;
the air seems thick and still. Then, lights blink on;
the escalators jerk and hum. And in the center, at
the exact center of the mall, a jet of water spurts

twenty feet straight up, then drops and spatters
in a shallow pool where signs announce that none
may ever go. O bright communion! O new cathedral!
where the appetitious, the impure, the old, the young,
the bored, the lost, the dumb, with wide dilated eyes
advance with offerings to be absolved and be made clean.
Now, the lime-lit chainlink fronts from over one hundred
pleasant and convenient stalls and stores are rolled away.
Now, odors of frying won tons come wafting up from
Lucy Ho's Bamboo Garden. And this music, always
everywhere, yet also somehow strangely played as if
not to be heard, pours its soft harangue down now.
The people wander forward now. And the world begins.

Adventures in Bronze

At the Will Rogers Court apartments
a young mother takes her toddler
into the living room to play,
then returns to the kitchen
to iron, and listen
to *Stella Dallas* on the radio.

Now the little one pushes at the front screen door,
finds it open, so stumbles out into the sun
where seven slightly older kids
come along, allowing him
to follow them
down the walk, down the road
to the old abandoned junior high
and the enormous, sunken, concrete storm drain there—
concrete smooth and cool,
concrete in the shade,
dark concrete the color
of Robert Oppenheimer's eyes
at any given moment in 1945.

The children climb down, scream, run around,
and so, with help, does the toddler too.
But then the older kids
climb out and run away,
climb out and leave the toddler alone.

The tips of his fingers can almost touch
the dead yellow grass
at the ground level top of the drain.

Soon enough he sees
there is nothing to do
except sit down on concrete and cry.

Soon enough he feels
there is nothing on earth
for him but this gray
and that blue rectangular swatch of sky.

From far far down the black tube of time
a man studies this scene in bronze.

A bronzed toddler is crying,
then looks up, seeing
first the head, then shoulders,
then the bronzed pedalpushers
of a bronzed mother there.

The man does not remember
the arms reaching up, or the arms reaching down,
just the distant sensation—
mendicant,
supplicant—
that he is risen,
that he inherits the air.

If I Could Open You

If I could open you, like
Einstein opened a hole
in the twentieth century,
that is what I would do.
When he realized what he
had done, I like to think he
sat there with his pencil, and
in his mind was a great, silver
city on a plain, and three
blue suns in the sky. And he
walked into that image then,
glad though terrified.

The Luncheon of the Boating Party

Under the red-and-white striped awning
extended over the restaurant porch,
the eyelids of these fourteen sundry revelers

seem to sag a bit, and that is because
by now they are all just a little drunk.
The party is as parties are. The people

are talking. Laughing. But in the upper
left-hand corner, a man wearing
a saffron straw hat, tilted jauntily down

over his brow, stands slightly apart
and silent against the thin balustrade.
This man stands with his back arched,

his chest out, and the large muscles
in his bare arms self-consciously flexed.
Certainly, he cannot be at ease, but then those

who desperately hope to be loved rarely are.
I say this because if one follows
the man's gaze across the top of the canvas,

across the party, to the upper right-hand corner,
one sees that he is, I believe, staring
at a young woman who has raised her hands

to adjust her hat or her hair, or to cover her ears
so as not to hear what the two men talking
to her are saying. The two men are smiling,

and one has taken the liberty of slipping
his arm round her waist. The young woman
is the only person in the boating party being

physically touched, and though she seems
oblivious to it, the man in the saffron hat
is not, and is not much amused by it either.

Then, as the eye roams over the rest
of the festive scene, the quiet joke of the artist
begins to emerge. For, although a half dozen

conversations continue on, half of these people
are not even seeing the person looking at them.
They are looking at somebody else. It is a sort

of visual quadrille, the theme of five hundred
French farces, except in this case the painter
must care very much for them all, for he has soothed

their wants and aches in a wash of softness.
I think he must have been a little drunk too.
But it is the eyes, these misty, wine-dark eyes

of the three women in the center of the painting,
that draw a viewer back again and again.
The women are looking at men. They are looking

that way women sometimes look
when they have had a little wine, and when
they are listening to someone in whose presence

they see no reason to be other than who they are,
someone to whom, as a matter of fact,
they wish to communicate how simple and gentle

life can sometimes be, how amniotic even,
as it seems to them now. It is not clear
if the men of the boating party perceive this,

or anything. To be honest, they seem selfish and vain.
But the artist sees it. And this is his gift,
this warm afternoon, his funny story to tell again

and again: a day of blue grapes and black wine, of tricks
of the eye, of the flow and lulls of time, and everything,
everything soaked in the light of sex and love and the sun.

The Lover Remembereth Such as He Sometime Enjoyed and Showeth How He Would Like to Enjoy Her Again

Luck is something I do not understand:
There were a lot of things I almost did
Last night. I almost went to hear a band
Down at The Swinging Door. I, almost, hid
Out in my room all night and read a book,
The Sot-Weed Factor, that I'd read before;
Almost, I drank a pint of Sunny Brook
I'd bought at the Dickson Street Liquor Store.

Instead I went to the Restaurant-On-The-Corner,
And tried to write, and did drink a beer or two.
Then coming back from getting rid of the beer,
I suddenly found I was looking straight at you.
Five months, my love, since I last touched your hand.
Luck is something I do not understand.

Morning Song

Flush and burn, your fever rose all night.
Your sleep was troubled; and even though I knew
This had to run its course, throughout the night
I tried but could not think of anything to do.
Often you cried out in that sleep, far away.
And wherever you were, I thought I could see
That whatever it was you kept wanting to say
It did not seem to have to do with me.

The tired eyes open. You see now that I see,
Swirling and tangled, inverted, how
In this firmament the blood streams and races.
Your smile and damp hair rush up to meet me,
Or is it I to them? This skin's blaze and glow—
The beads of dew on these most secret places.

Semi-Sentimental Thank You Note Sent over a Long Distance

Let me tell you
    I'm still trying
        to cope with
    the disappointment. All
I wanted for Christmas
    was a scratch-and-
        sniff photo
    of you amongst
some clover. Instead
    this book of the fifty
        worst movies
    ever made. And a box
of pink erasers? Maybe
    I'm slow but I
        don't get it. Oh
    yes I know we are
separated by that
    enormously faded
        and dirty spread-out
    serape, that distinctive
state of mind, Oklahoma—
    but down here I am
        left mostly to
    my own devices. Here,
like Jackie Gleason's red
    satin bowling shirt,
        I lack subtlety
    and stand too much out
in the crowd. So
    what I am getting at,
        what I am trying
    to say, my little
lotus blossom, my little
    dove of Canaan, my

little garbanzo
bean, is thanks a lot
but I really must ask you
to get up off that
divine rotundity, your
ass, and send that
clever clover photo
right on down
the line right
now. There exists
a definite need! Like
Jackie Gleason's bowling
shirt, sooner
or later, I'm headed
your way, and when
I get back to Arkansas,
either to pick
you up or stay, let's
both plan on working
hard at, O ho, seeing
ah, eye to eye,
et al, and I might
add, toe to toe, et
al, nose to nose,
O, thigh to
thigh, et al,
ah, O, well, yes, O.

A Skeptical View of the Tarot

The Purveyor to the Czar attended a new exhibition
of post-impressionist efforts by Lonzo,
a recent twinkle in the art world sky.
The important official paused before
one painting, and said it gave *him*
the impression of the dried egg yellow
he found on his fork at breakfast that morning.
The next canvas, he said, gave him the impression
of his courtesan's black lace panties
lying on the carpet that afternoon,
a sour fog hovering over them, almost visible.

Lonzo, holding a skeptical view of the Tarot,
having, for the occasion, arrayed himself as The Fool
carrying a white rose and strolling over a cliff,
an ironic gesture of defiance,
heard these things.

As the purveyor continued his ridicule,
moving from painting to painting,
the locked stalls of the flaming mules
of melancholy were opened wide,
causing horrible screams to be heard in the land.
Then the artist was filled with dark choler,
saw the flaw in his gesture, and considered
that perhaps, after all, his chosen garb
did correctly express his archetype.

This Other

Your self confronts you at the oddest times.
   Not too often, but often at odd times,
this other bangs through the front door, catching
   you tired and at supper, but still in your black
cape and doublet, tired, of imagining
   knowing, of imagining gesturing
hypnotically from the battlements,—
   and your dinner becomes an interrupted
dinner, as he sits down and digs into
   the roast duck, orange sauce, the red Bordeaux.

You think: what a strange fellow. A healthy
   appetite, but the little paper pirate hat
sitting on his head, the kind in the dime stores
   around Halloween, would put most people off.
He eats with his hands. Quickly. And yet,
   there is something about this ruffian,
something about this greasy gorilla,
   something about this person with a penchant
for orange sauce, that makes you think: here is one
   with which I might dine; one with which I might
lift a fine glass; one with which I might speak.

A Funny Joke

A man fell out of grace.
It was my father.

On the north slope of Alaska,
on land belonging to

the Atlantic-Richfield Oil Corporation,
he fell.

He lay there six hours.
Then he was found.

Three hours later,
the Atlantic-Richfield Oil Corporation

flew him to Fairbanks
where doctors were.

They said he was ill.
They said the way

his face, arm, leg, in fact
his whole left side

was drawn up
in a hideous, contorted,

spasm of paralysis
meant he was in ill health.

My brother was there.
My brother said

this was what was in my father's eyes:
fear.

My brother said
his mouth was twisted

into a permanent ghastly grin.
It looked always as if

his was the only smile around,
as if someone had told

the funniest joke finally,
but only he had heard

and we were unaware,
there, that last day

my father was an employee
of the Atlantic-Richfield Oil Corporation.

The Drifting Away of All We Once Held Essential

Now here's the truth: there is a tide in the affairs
of men. And it will drag your ass right out
to sea and dump you, if you aren't careful.
In October, in Texas, in a room, in a city,
the stylist sat, working on his book, *Strange
Things along the Rio Grande,* a comparative study
of masturbatory techniques and tendencies
of certain southern oral-interpretation-of-literature
professors and South Texas redneck barflies.
But a seemingly insurmountable impasse
has been reached in the project, of late,
due to the almost complete refusal
of the barflies to answer the more pertinent portions
of his questionnaire. God! God! It all at once
made him think somehow, he knew not how,
of the day when he was just a jerk of a lad:
a page, a pup, a whelp, a wag, a sprite, a recent
winner of the Baby Leroy Look-Alike Contest, and he had
asked the doctor where these latest acquisitions, these
hemorrhoids, had come from. And he, misunderstanding,
thought the doctor said he must have recently had
a *hard stew.* And the doctor laughed laughed laughed
in his face, upon hearing him reply that he
hadn't had any stew at all in months. It, all at once,
made him think of kleptomania somehow, and what
a joy it had been to him in his younger days.
Question: is it true that, when the stylist
was thirteen, he had taken the whole fourteen dollars
he had made from selling Boy Scout peanut brittle
and spent it in one afternoon at the movies,
returning home with only a giant glue-together
plastic model of a bumblebee, some already fading
memories of the cyclops in *The Seventh
Voyage of Sinbad,* and the blood sugar level
of a terminal alcoholic, caused by

washing down nine candy bars with three
chocolate malts? And is it also true that, one week
later, on their drive to the scout meeting
where the previously mentioned funds were to be
turned in, the child stylist informed his father
of what he had done, thus causing his father
to become distressed? Thus causing his father
to almost cry, saying over and over, "What did
we do wrong? What did we do wrong?" And
is it not the case that the child did
cry at that point in time, but in ecstasy,
as the father lent him the money he needed,
as they drove along, the child crying there beside him
in the dark? Answer: yes, all that's just as real
as a red rag; and it marvels the stylist, to this day,
with what complete vividness that scene, from
so many years gone by, can be called up for purposes
of flagellation, from the darker regions
to rip and tear at the pink soft underbelly of thought.
Look at them there: father and son, driving
along. So close. Real pals. My
God! What a load of crap! Kleptomania! Fuck! Shit!
Cunt! Piss! A whole family of Lone Rangers! That's
what it was! Masked Avengers! The William Tell
Overture ad infinitum. We flew our flag: *Don't
Tread on Me.* And if you did, then you'd see
such venom. I will do such things! I will steal
such things! What they are I know not. But I do know
Hold me Daddy and whip me Daddy, and turn
your distant eyes at last on me. See, I did
this and took this and this. Hold me. . . .
The stylist paused. Put down his pen. His eyes ran
dry. Tired. His mind was tired. But there was so much
still to do. He really had so very much to do.
He really must finish this latest project, this
attempt to add to the body of total knowledge in the world.

A Few Words for Frank Stanford: 1948–1978

We live awhile. And then
　　we die. "The first
time I saw you, I thought
　　you was bald," he said
to me. I checked my head,
　　to see if he was right.

Of all things to recall
　　on this first birthday
of this death, that was
　　the first to come along.

1.　*The Tale*
Back when a few of us others would gather together,
the red steaks on, the cheap wine rolling down,
we would tell the true, the oft-repeated story
of the summer Frank worked on Sam's surveying crew.

　　One day they stopped for lunch out in the woods
　　where they had been clearing brush almost since dawn.
　　After a while, Frank jumped up with no warning,
　　stripped, grabbed his machete and ran off into the trees
　　hacking, screaming, over and over, "I
　　am physically superior! Mentally superior! I
　　am spiritually superior to anybody here!"
　　Now, the ones who happened to be *there*
　　were Sam, and two semi-illiterates sucking Skoal.
　　One spit, and said, "That boy is a weird one.
　　You got to admit he's a hell of a worker though."

And then we'd laugh and drink, devour, and drink
some more. Laughter and liquor seemed much the same
back then. Each of us cramming deep inside the fact
that possibly Frank had meant some other thing:

that possibly Frank had attempted to convey
that when he said *here,* he didn't mean *there,* but
here, us, with our wine. And the thing that stung
in our little selves, our so young selves,
our enormous, ignorant, frightened selves:
we thought possibly what he had to say was true,—
or, more than that, maybe, possibly, probably, true.

2.   *His House*
It fell to us to clean the sick mess up,—
so we drove over, slid up into his yard
and parked the car. The honeysuckle stank.
The door was open and every light was on.
It looked like somebody had left in a hurry:
the house was empty, but every light was on.

There was a little blood on the bed, a little
blood smeared on the phone and that was all.
The house was empty. We stood around.

                                             Frank,
while I was flying back from Houston
you effected a definite, permanent change,
and every light was on. This was the home
where a man had taken a gun and blown and blown
and blown his being away three hours before
I never knew what silence was, Frank,
until I walked through that door

3.
He cared for *Wise Blood.*
    He cared for Cocteau.
For *Rashomon.* A man obsessed
    by his own adoption,
"There are two people

inside of me," he said.
"I don't know who I am," he
    told me, drunk and sad,—
but not, I think, entirely so.

He acquired, through the years,
    devoted disciples not
to be denied. Near the end,
    when he was in debt, when he
thought he was immortal,
    when he had arrived
at a country where
    others could scream and
call and he could not
    hear, there, near the end,
near that ragged, barren,
    ignorant, excessive end,
we did not get along. But
    I feel now I must say:
"When he sat down at a desk
    the juice crackled and came.
He could write about
    moonlight. He could write
about swine. He could
    write about starfish,
lunchmeat, Memphis,
    minnows and bay rum,
Robert Desnos. He had
    the blue flow. He had
the red hand. My God,
    he had the touch, my friends."

Those are the final words
    on this ridiculous day:

he had the touch, my friends.
　When a world winds down
there need be none but those.
　Never, never, never,
no words but those. Except
　perhaps, "We live awhile."

So, bring women to sing,
　and to cover him over
with white sheets of paper.

Bring roses to deaden
　the clods as they fall.

Airport Bars

1.
Like shoveling in linguini
while listening to *Bolero*
at dinner last night,
and like swilling down martinis
between flights tonight,
things are gaining speed.

In the rain outside,
they taxi, roll and rise.

Does everything always depart
and does nothing remain?

These big windows, and the way
the wind flings its wet against them,
the way, far down, people outside
are blown around in silence,
the way their flashlights flicker on
then off, in silence, blinking
asterisks in blackness, and how
the people speak in silence,
the lips move, but without sound,
reminds me, for a moment,
of a silent film I saw once
called *Orphans of the Storm*.
But only for a moment, then—
it goes.
Swilling down martinis.

Do memories always depart?
It seemed that in that movie
people were always buffeted about
by great but natural forces,

when all they really wanted—
and not with much success—
was to hold their ground,
or get back to where they came from,
or make a little headway
toward some vaguely distant town
over the horizon.

Where are the peach-tinted sunsets,
the green summer twilights,
those sidewalks on which
I smeared *Jane Poshataske*
in lightning bug, luminous,
chartreuse, phosphor, fading away?
God, the things that return,
that we wish would remain,
like resurrected Romanovs
laying claim for a while
to a throne long gone, but they fade—
pinpoints of light, they fade,
stains on the dark, they fade,
leaving only the far, slate wall
of what is still to be. And that wall
is speeding up. It is moving this way.

2.
And if memories stayed? How would that be?
Cautiously,
carefully, of such should we dream,
for most of the time
welling up come back things
that seem more like Shakespearean ghosts
than like twilights, golden or green,
ghosts full of prophecy, banshees, old trolls

with gnarled knuckles, grabbing hold
and being loath to let go—
fungi, of sorts, but no,
almost never those beautiful twilights.
Of that I am sure.

3.
It was one of those
"Golden Age" TV variety hours
that started each week with caricatures
of twenty or thirty of the biggest stars
distorted but recognizably drawn—
then each week one or two would appear.

Martha Raye's mouth was as big
as her head, but it was
JIMMY DURANTE
that caught his eye—
because in the rendering the artist had done
JIMMY DURANTE
had a sausage for a nose,
a foot-long sausage, fat and round.

He asked his father if that was so.
"Oh, Jesus yes:
JIMMY DURANTE
has a huge nose."

And so the boy felt, "If somewhere that
could somehow be—
well, maybe the world really is a wonder—
and not what it seems."

Then the night they announced that the host that week
would be The-One-And-Only!

Mr. Ink-A-Dink-A-Doo!
The Old Schnozzola!
a rush of joy
slid along his spine—
and a soft, slow thunder wandered through his mind.

Then this ugly old guy danced out—
and at that exact instant
a glimpse of The Essence
was portioned out
for the boy to see:
a loud old man, a total ass.
But no sausage anywhere to be seen.

His father looked over,
noticed the frown,
the reek, the faint auras
of disgust and disappointment
swirling.

"Ha ha!" the father said. "Close,
but no kielbasa. Ha ha!" the father said.
"Close, but no cigar."

4.
And so we sit here, Gentle Reader,
halfway between two places,
looking for a little satinity
to ease the slide;
not knowing anyone
for many miles around,
but feeling, for no discernible cause,
My Gracious Peruser-Of-This-Page,
an inability to be laid-back about it,
the self-same consciousness a man feels

when he finds himself alone in a room,
swilling down martinis,
and begins to act out
all the things he might have said.
Then someone comes in, stands behind him,
catching him there with his finger in the air.

Robert Rickert Wrote Back

the roll, the rise, the carol . . .
—Hopkins

Robert Rickert wrote back, saying,
"Too many dead days in a row? Dost thou

not dwell near the sea? Shut up. Take
walks by the shore. Jesus. Get out.

Spend time beneath trees." And so today
I walked on the beach. And the clouds hung

over the sea made the sea look like
one, enormous, heaving mass of

impure mercury. I thought, "How
lovely." And then, "How lovely to say

lovely." "It heaps me!" I claimed.
Then the dream came. A gargoyle

facing my face. My arm striking hard,
carving. Let me cut the flare of this

nostril right! Deep shoulder pain.
Chips of gray stone in my hair. Birds

whirling round. My self on a rock roof
one hundred feet above ground. Let

me carve this flare! Face powdered
with stone dust and now rain beginning

beginning to cake my hair. But nothing
mattering but the flare. The ache

clean, cut clean, rain clean. The
flare! Then the gargoyle gives out,

retches rain from the spout of its mouth,
down over tongue and teeth, down

crashing and washing my face, my hair.
And that was the end. End of the dream.

Was all.—I came back to the beach,
back to the soft, meaningless mantra,

the tide at my feet. Today, by the shore,
an unction. A dream of waking. To confront

and carve stone. Make mirrors in stone.
Gargoyles only some god would ever see.

Chance of Showers

for Matt Horan

Like the greatest steak house
salad bar you ever saw, there is some-
   thing varied but, I am afraid, all
too familiar in this big autumnal air.

And yet, what other season
boils up such aches to get it down
   precisely, hoping to avoid again
the always striking, but also fatal,

   mention of the ornithological
V's on high. The trees seem the color
   of fire trucks or blood or rust
again, but why? Why do we recall

   the things we do? "Why did
the little moron take hay to bed?" I
   don't suppose a week has passed
in thirty years I have not asked myself

   that question. Why? Like-
wise with Billy Pinzer. I was only
   two, but every week I waddle out
on the porch once more, and see Billy

   in the front yard, holding a little
yellow metal roadster. Ah Billy, he is
   my buddy. He smiles at me. I
smile at him. I walk up to him. He hits

   me in the face with the roadster.
Sometimes, when I peer out at my freshman
   class, those seats of desolation,
or when I hear some Texan say something

particularly inane, I think
Billy is behind these bombs bursting
    in here that, for an instant,
cause me to consider flipping through

    advertisements in the back
of *Argosy*—to order a used, an actual
    Colombian machete. "Imagine
the expressions on your friends' faces

    as you cut a bloody swathe
through the gang." For an instant.
    Then I take another sip of coffee,
lean back and keep my mouth quite shut.

    So does form give meaning
to memory. Does memory give meaning
    to form? "Why yes!" cried crazy
Vera so long ago her face flared up

    today from some recess where I
thought just narcosis reigned, miasmal
    and malign. I got older this year,
and like black lightning from a blue sky

    it surprised the hell out
of me. I don't think I could honestly
    describe things as looking up,
but I can say they are still looking

    not dull. Mortality, who
would have thought it? Maybe the best
    to be hoped for is to pop off
in mid-melody, like Bach. These random

cameos, however, and tableaux
on parade appear preferable to even
    the best of last refrains now.
For now. Now this glass wherein I see

    myself lets me see other things
as well. That window in the far
    wall, for instance, and outside
houses dripping gingerbread on the hill

    across the street. If I squint
hard enough, they seem a rocky misty
    blue-gray panorama, like
the inaccessible backgrounds of certain

    Renaissance portraits of great
renown. Although I must say those craggy
    backgrounds always made me think:
"That girl had better get going if she

    wants to be home by dark."
Hogs are among us, no doubt about it,
    no hedge against inflation
either. Ben Kimpel tells me things come

    in cycles, I suppose that means
circles, and I guess that is a type
    of good news, but I don't know, these
recollections seem constant, growing, one

    long craggy protean scene,
and my bad knee gets worse every year,
    I use it to forecast the weather
now, stuff to feed my nightmares and

daymares. My parents singing
"Always." While the shish kebab sellers,
    on the corners and streets
of the world, are not moved to tears.

The Party's End

The moon steered a rusty car away.

We wandered into the backyard.

There was a little wind.

Someone sad whispered, "See,
now the poem of joy comes striding."

And I saw it then.

Why did it come then,
through the dirty horse of the night?

What visions came?

I saw my father working.
He bent and fell in Alaskan snow.

My brother also fell.

I wanted to touch them then.
I believe
I wanted to scream, "Help me,
God! Immensity!
Let me come unto you.
Let me come unto
you. Let me
come unto you."

But, of course,
none of us said anything.

The dawn was there.

And I was cold.

And all rage left me.

A frost had collected
on the shingles, and the grass,
so lovely
to my drunken eyes.

Señor Wences and the Man in the Box

L. B. Stokesbury (1924–1987)

Jokester, prankster, petty gangster, son,
let me see you laugh your way out of this one.
No one should know better than you
except maybe now me, that there is no word, no posy,
no black scratch on the white eyeball of blankness,
no pisshole in snow, that can capture
for even an instant
what anyone really is at any time.
                                        And so,
and even so, laddybuck, my little Sisyphus,
prankster, son, I lie here now
blessed to watch your scared frown staring down.

And what did you expect? Some hideous
blaming rictus glaring back? What you deserved
for the thousand times you flashed
that crappy gaze of yours
that said I owed you something
obligatory, a gift I never gave? Oh
no. Not me. And not here, assuredly. No.

But if I do owe you something, if there is
a remembrance that you might in faith require,
some faint sachet to hold before the nose in future years,
maybe this will do:
last night, myself sequestered here,
my cheeks having taken on a certain pale,
no longer imbued
with their usual natural cutaneous hue
but with white rather,
ash white, whale
white, lead white, dare I say
dead white, while I was just
lying here extremely still, cold toes

saluting the North Star,
a pimply boy I never in my life had seen before
stepped softly up and violently
massaged the muscles of my cheek and jaw.
Then he jammed a piece of plastic,
a sort of warped elongated
MasterCard, in each corner of my mouth
between the lip and gum. Then
with a slick, quick, solid push and pull
he popped the plastic out, leaving
this look I lie here with today:
this look you are staring at right now:
a look they label as *serene.*

How's that? OK? You can have it.
On the house. A nosegay.

Ah, laddybuck, if we could have found
some demilitarized zone, which we could not;
if I could for once
have raised you up out of your maze of corridors,
which I could not; you
with your boxcars of words words words:
little links of ink lined up, all in a row, chugging
off toward the horizon; maybe then
I could have told you what you wanted to hear.

Instead, only this:
myself, disassembling, desirous to consign
my pressing embassy, that would have come,
could have come, should have come
sooner, I concede.
Myself, answering, Sisyphus, son,
the lid coming down now

ash white,
better late than never answering, ending thus
this last refrain, jokester, prankster,
son, just a tiny crack left now:

It's all right.

Notes

"Evening's End": "Summertime" was written by George and Ira Gershwin in 1935. Big Brother and the Holding Company recorded its version of the song for the Columbia Records album *Cheap Thrills* in 1968.

The Royal Nonesuch: See *The Adventures of Huckleberry Finn*, chapters 22–23.

"Felliniesque": Most of the imagery in this poem was suggested by Fellini's film *8½*, which was released in 1963 and starred Marcello Mastroianni.

Autumn Rhythm: Autumn Rhythm, painted in 1950 by Jackson Pollock, is part of the permanent collection of the Metropolitan Museum of Art in New York City.

"This Print of Dürer's": "The Knight, Death, and the Devil" is an engraving completed by Albrecht Dürer in 1513. One print hangs in the Frick Museum in New York City.

Footlight Parade: Directed by Lloyd Bacon and Busby Berkeley in 1933, this film starred James Cagney, Joan Blondell, Dick Powell, and Ruby Keeler.

The Luncheon of the Boating Party: "Le Déjeuner des Canotiers," completed by Pierre Auguste Renoir in 1881, is part of the permanent collection of the Phillips Gallery in Washington, D.C.

"Señor Wences and the Man in the Box": *Señor Wences* is the name of a popular ventriloquist who often appeared on the television program "The Ed Sullivan Show," during the 1950s and 1960s.